DOODLES at LUNCH

DEBORAH ZEMKE

Blue Apple Books

1) Draw a sideways A.

2) Add four curls . . .

3) three bumpy lines . . .

4) legs with claws . . .

5) six curved lines . . .

6) eyes and teeth.

Doodle an ALLIGATOR with an A

Alligators have strong, sharp teeth. But they don't chew their food, they snatch and swallow. Gulp!

©2009 Deborah Zemke

Doodle a **BUTTERFLY** with a B

Mmmmm, what smells so good? To sniff out flowers with tasty nectar, a butterfly follows its nose—which is on its antennae on top of its head.

©2009 Deborah Zemke

It's the flight of the bumble B!

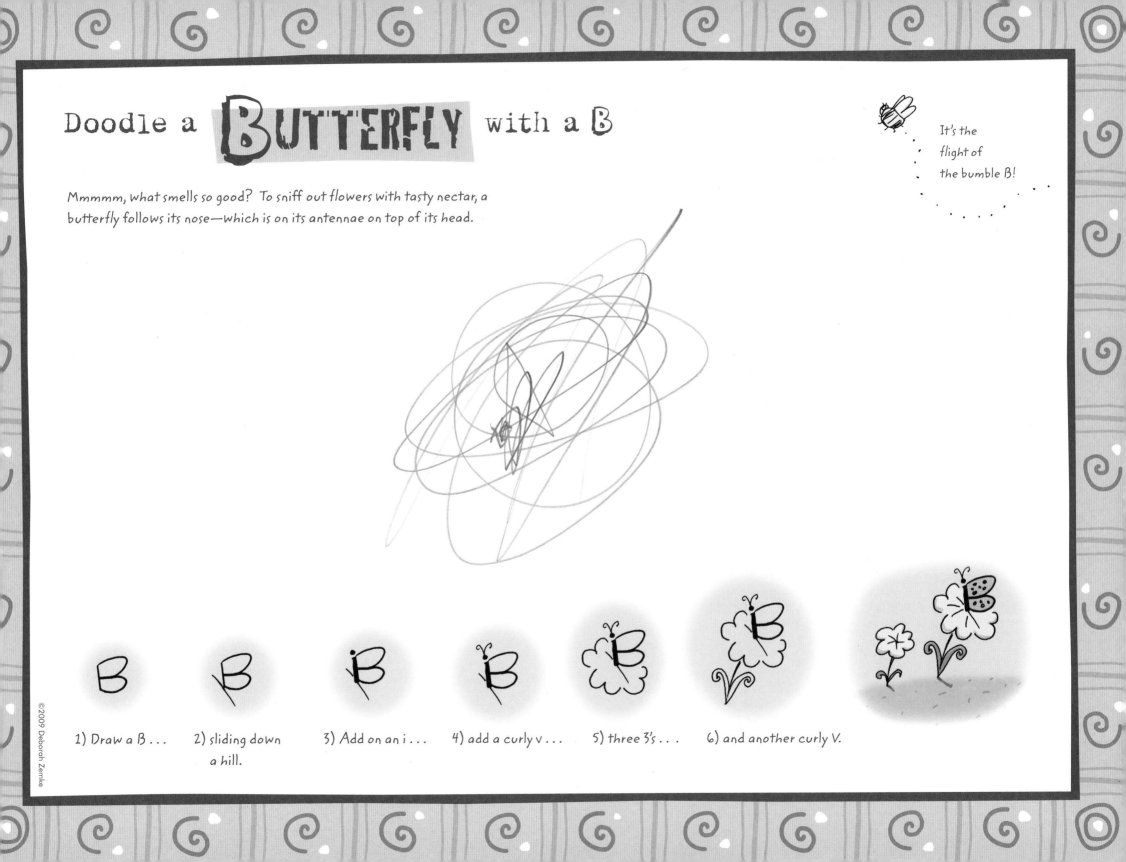

1) Draw a B . . .

2) sliding down a hill.

3) Add on an i . . .

4) add a curly v . . .

5) three 3's . . .

6) and another curly V.

1) Draw a C . . .

2) and a backward C.

3) Add two fat triangles . . .

4) eight skinny ones . . .

5) and ten trapezoids.

6) Draw ten more triangles . . .

7) two ziggy V's . . .

8) and finally, claws and eyes!

Doodle a

CRAB

with a C

Crabs walk sideways because that's the direction that their legs bend. But they can see all the way around since their two eyes swivel on stalks.

1) Draw four swinging d's.

 2) Make two big waves, one of them upside down.

 3) Add a small black T . . .

 4) two O's with dots . . .

 5) two flying teardrops . . .

 6) and three slices.

Doodle a **DOG** with a **D** Dogs are loyal, eager, hardworking, and hungry!

Doodle an  ELEPHANT with an E

An elephant's trunk may look like a giant straw but it works more like a hose. The elephant fills its trunk with water and then pours the water into its mouth.

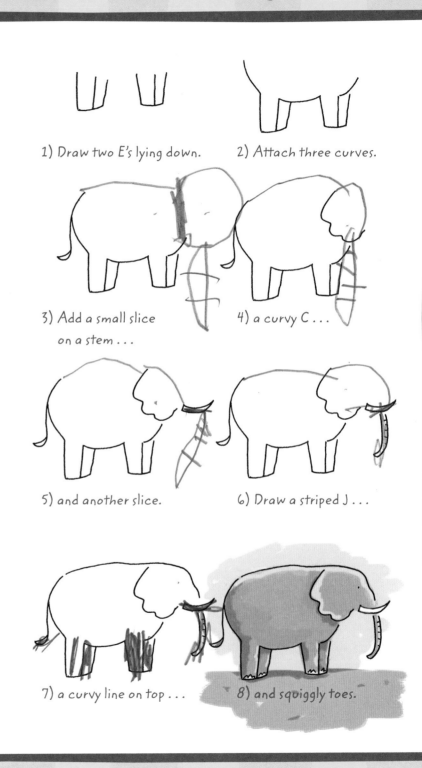

1) Draw two E's lying down.

2) Attach three curves.

3) Add a small slice on a stem . . .

4) a curvy C . . .

5) and another slice.

6) Draw a striped J . . .

7) a curvy line on top . . .

8) and squiggly toes.

Doodle a Fox with an F

Here I am! A fox uses its bushy tail like a flag to signal other foxes.

1) Draw an F.
2) Attach a C.   *These flags are flying!*
3) Add a bean . . .
4) three triangles . . .
5) and three dots.
6) Make rows of squiggles . . .
7) legs and . . .
8) the tip of the tail.

1) Draw a G.

2) Make a face of two O's, a C, and a J.

3) Add a rounded M . . .

4) and two topsy-turvy V's.

5) Add a W and some hair . . .

but not too much.

6) Give Grandpa hands and feet . . .

7) twinkling eyes . . .

and a dotted bowtie.

Gee! The goose is loose!

Doodle a GRANDPA with a G

What does your grandpa like to eat for lunch?

 1) Draw an h lying down.

 2) Attach a D . . .

3) and a P lying down.

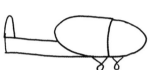 4) Add two v's and two o's . . .

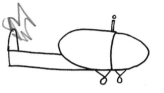 5) a dotted i . . .

6) and three skinny triangles to take off!

Doodle a **HELICOPTER** with an **H**

Helicopters can fly up, down, backwards, and sideways and hang in mid-air. It's all in the rotor blades that work like spinning wings.

Doodle an **INSECT** with an i

Insects rule! There are more insects than any other creature on earth— and they all have six legs, no more and no less.

1) Draw two i's...

2) on top of an O.

3) Add two dotted O's.

4) Attach a small W.

5) Add two big O's...

6) three i's leaning left...

7) and six i's upside down.

Here's a bright idea!

I scream for ice cream!

Doodle a  JAGUAR with a J

Like most cats, jaguars love to eat fish! But unlike other cats, they're good swimmers and don't mind getting wet to catch a tasty meal.

1) Draw four swinging j's.

2) Make four squiggly paws . . .

3) and attach three big waves.

4) Attach a U . . .

5) a question mark . . .

6) and connect them with a swoop.

7) Draw a slanted Y on a black T . . .

8) two V's, a double curve, two small o's . . .

9) and swirly spots.

Kangaroos don't need to drink much or often, but when they're thirsty, they'll dig in the ground until they find water.

Doodle a
KANGAROO
with a K

7) then draw curly toes, eyes and nose.

1) Draw a leaning K.

2) Add two curvy V's...

3) two question marks...

4) two 2's...

5) and four tears.

6) Attach a big C...

1) Draw a leaning L.

2) Add a d and a triangle . . .

3) rows of squiggly mane . . .

4) seven L's and a 2 . . .

5) connected by a bean.

6) Now add a tail with a tear . . .

7) four loopy paws . . .

8) and teeth!

Doodle a **LION** with an **L**

Lions roar to say "Get lost!" They rub cheeks with each other to say "Hi."

1) Spell the word -- m start with m . . .

2) add an O . . .

3) and a U . . .

4) a skinny S . . .

5) and an e.

6) Now add eyes, feet, whiskers . . .

7) and some tasty cheese!

©2009 Deborah Zemke

Doodle a **MOUSE** with an **M**

Cheese, shmeese. Mice would rather eat chocolate.

Doodle a **NEWT** with an **N**

1) Draw two n's.
2) Attach two eyes . . .
3) and a y.
4) Add two V's, an N, and a Z.
5) Draw loopy fingers . . .
6) a curvy tail . . .
7) and stripes.

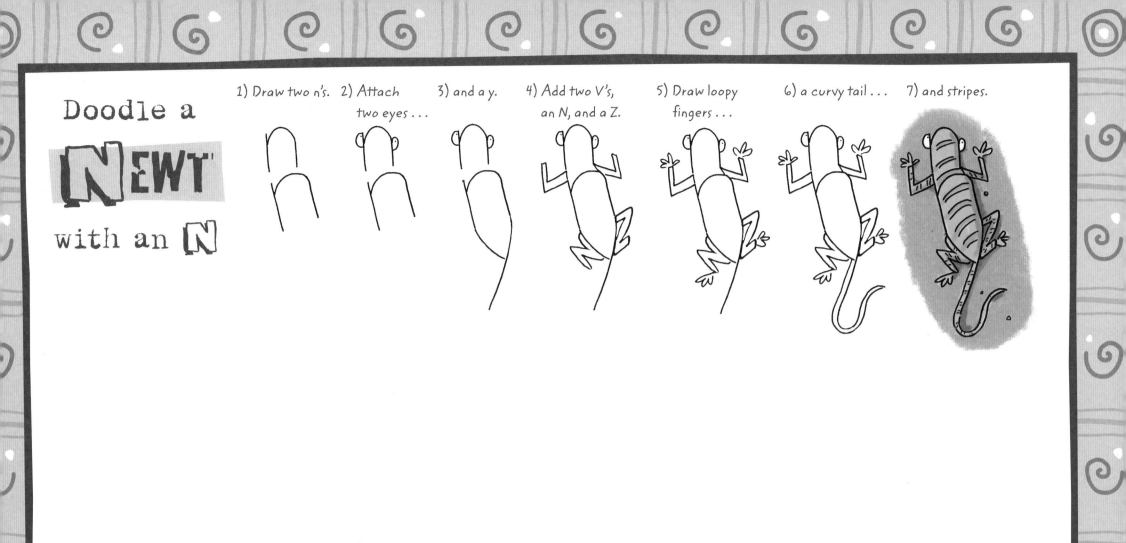

Newts, like frogs and salamanders, are amphibians.
They spend the first part of their lives living in water and the second living on land.

Doodle an OCTOPUS with an O

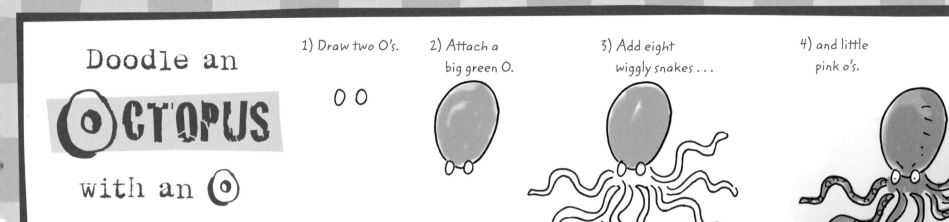

1) Draw two O's.

O O

2) Attach a big green O.

3) Add eight wiggly snakes . . .

4) and little pink o's.

With a big head and eight arms, the octopus is one of the smartest and strangest creatures in the sea. It can change its color, pattern and texture to match its surroundings. It squirts ink, collects shells, and can regrow an arm if it loses one.

Doodle a PTERODACTYL with a P

Is it a bird? Is it a plane? It's a reptile! But don't go looking for one of these flying lizards today—
they've been extinct for millions of years.

1) Draw a flying p.

2) Add a topsy-turvy V . . .

3) and a J . . .

4) and three
lines.

5) Attach a
big C . . .

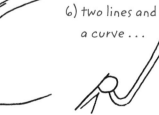

6) two lines and
a curve . . .

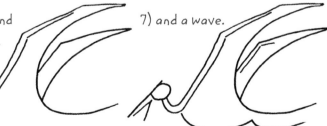

7) and a wave.

Doodle a QUARTERBACK with a Q

The quarterback on a football team plays a lot—and studies a lot. He needs to know every play and where every player is going to be on the field.

1) Draw a Q.

2) Add a striped trapezoid . . .

3) and a big fat T.

4) Draw a square W . . .

5) two L's . . .

6) a hand holding a football . . .

7) and a hand pointing to a touchdown.

Doodle a **ROBOT** with an R

Beep, beep! I, Robot. I hungry. I eat electricity.

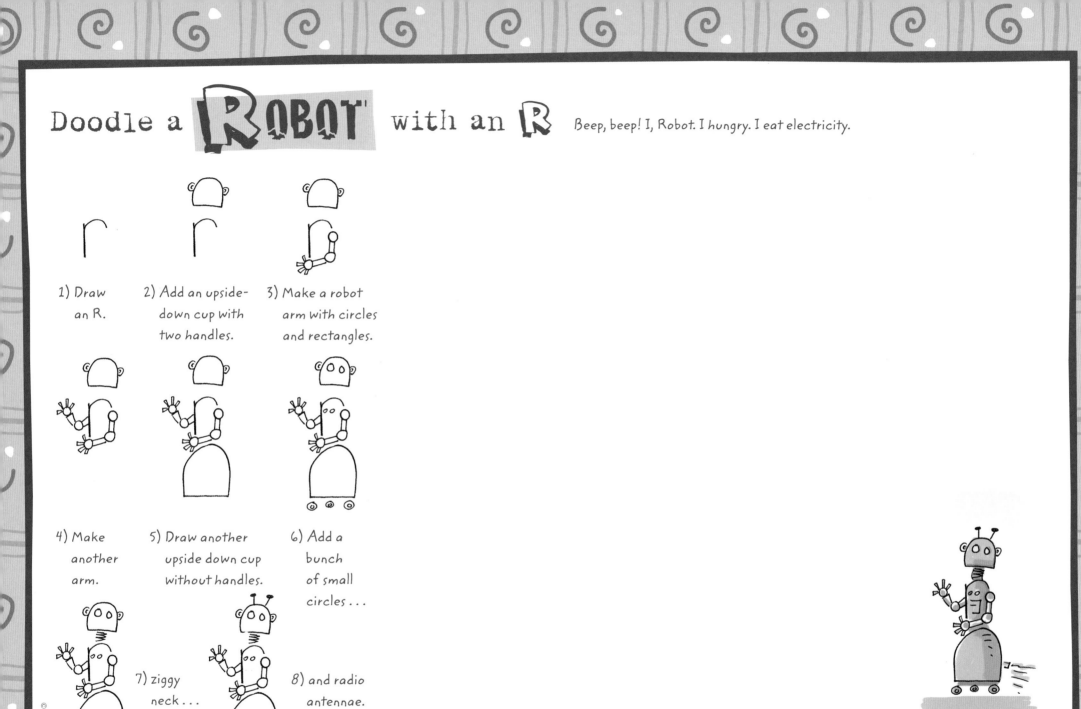

1) Draw an R.

2) Add an upside-down cup with two handles.

3) Make a robot arm with circles and rectangles.

4) Make another arm.

5) Draw another upside down cup without handles.

6) Add a bunch of small circles . . .

7) ziggy neck . . .

8) and radio antennae.

9) Now watch your robot go!

©2009 Deborah Zemke

Doodle a  SEAHORSE with an S

With a head like a horse, bony armor instead of scales, and a curled tail with no fin, seahorses don't look like any other fish. Some are as small as the fingernail on your little pinky.

1) Draw an S...

2) crossed by short lines.

3) Add wavy lines.

4) Add two waves.

5) Make a big curve...

6) a curvy snout...

7) and a dotted O eye.

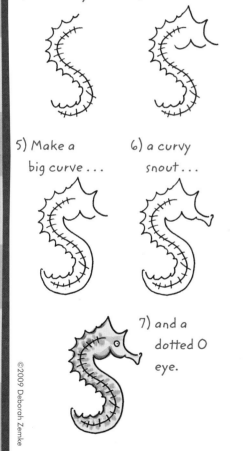

©2009 Deborah Zemke

Supper is smokin'.

How many S's are on this plate of spaghetti?

It's a sssssssssnake.

Doodle a

-REX

with a T

The biggest meat eater
of all time, Tyrannosaurus
Rex grew to twenty feet tall.
Its head was six feet long.

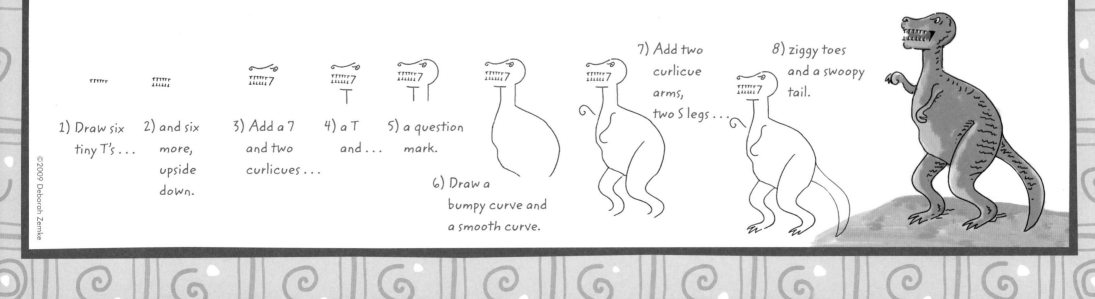

1) Draw six
tiny T's . . .

2) and six
more,
upside
down.

3) Add a 7
and two
curlicues . . .

4) a T
and . . .

5) a question
mark.

6) Draw a
bumpy curve and
a smooth curve.

7) Add two
curlicue
arms,
two S legs . . .

8) ziggy toes
and a swoopy
tail.

Doodle an UMBRELLA with a U

The first umbrellas were used over 4,000 years ago in Egypt. Why would they need umbrellas where there is so little rain? To protect people from the sun.

1) Draw a fat U.

2) Attach four U's on top . . .

3) and a little U on the bottom.

4) Draw four waves.

5) Add an l.

6) Put an upside down U on top.

7) Now pick it up and turn it around before you get wet!

Doodle a **VAMPIRE BAT** with a ♥

1) Draw two small v's.

V V

2) Add an upside down heart . . .

3) inside another upside down heart.

4) Draw two v's on sticks.

5) Hang your bat from a branch and finish with three dots and fur.

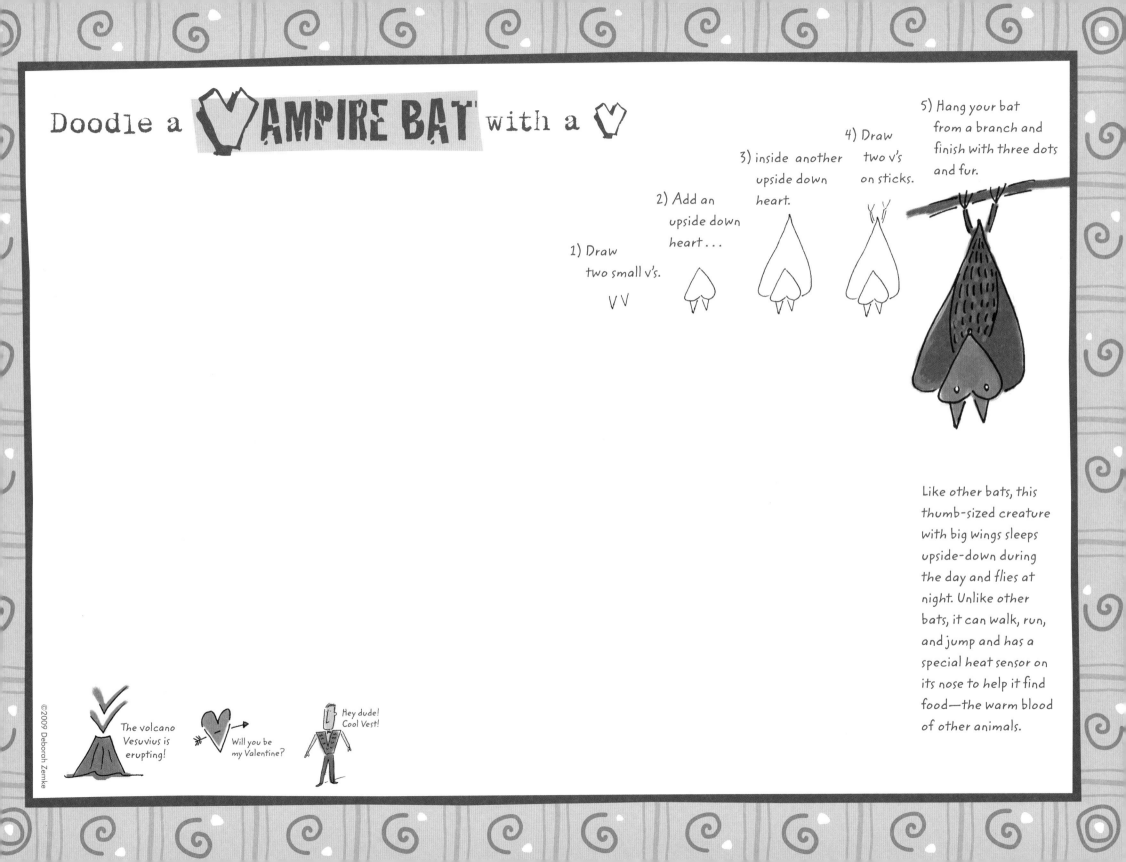

Like other bats, this thumb-sized creature with big wings sleeps upside-down during the day and flies at night. Unlike other bats, it can walk, run, and jump and has a special heat sensor on its nose to help it find food—the warm blood of other animals.

The volcano Vesuvius is erupting!

Will you be my Valentine?

Hey dude! Cool Vest!

Doodle a **WALRUS** with a W

What's for lunch? If you're a walrus it's clams—thousands of clams. But those huge front teeth aren't used as clam openers. A walrus uses its two tusks to haul itself out of the water.

1) Draw a tall, skinny W.

2) Top it with an upside down wave.

3) Add a question mark . . .

4) one d and one b . . .

5) two sideways V's . . .

6) and a big J.

7) Now make flippers with four curly V's.

Doodle an  X-RAY FISH with an X

You can actually see inside this transparent fish. But you have to take a really close look because x-ray fish are only two inches long.

1) Draw an X.

2) Connect the ends.

3) Add an arrow.

4) Connect with curves.

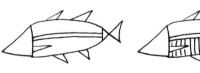

5) Add five triangles . . .

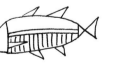

6) stripes . . .

7) a row of X's . . .

8) eyes and speckles.

Doodle a YO-YO with a Y

Come back! That's what the word yo-yo means. It comes from the Philippines, where people hunted with giant yo-yos.

©2009 Deborah Zemke

1) Draw a y with a long tail.

2) Attach an O.

3) Add four curls . . .

4) a bow . . .

5) and a striped J.

6) Draw a striped trapezoid . . .

7) a squared W . . .

8) and a self-portrait.

1) Draw six skinny Z's.

2) Add two question marks.

3) Put an S on one . . .

4) and two teardrops on the other.

5) Draw a swervy S . . .

6) four skinny striped V legs . . .

7) with wedge feet.

8) Add a ziggy mane . . .

9) and four blue Z's. Good night, zebra!

Doodle a
ZEBRA
with a Z

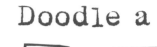

No two zebras are striped exactly alike, but they look so much alike that a lion has a hard time picking out just one to chase. And every zebra is ready for the chase—they can run one hour after they're born!

Doodle a LADYBUG with a 1

Ladybugs lead short but hungry lives— in six weeks a ladybug may eat 5,000 plant-eating insects, so gardeners love to invite ladybugs to lunch.

9) and spots!

1) Write 1.

2) Add a curve on one side . . .

3) and another curve on the other side.

4) Put two curves on top . . .

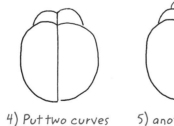

5) another one on top of that . . .

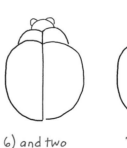

6) and two more curves on top of that.

7) Add two curlicues . . .

8) six angle legs . . .

1) Draw a 2.

2) Add a loop . . .

3) and a curve . . .

4) and a leaf-shaped wing.

5) Draw another curve in front . . .

6) and attach a squiggly line on the bottom.

7) Add a pointy tail.

8) Make this duck a green-headed Mallard!

What's for lunch? Do plants, bugs and slugs sound yummy? They would if you were a duck!

Doodle a  DUCK with a 2

Doodle a ISH with a 3

Would you like a 1,500 pound tuna fish sandwich for lunch?
That's how big a bluefin tuna can grow!

1) Draw a 3 . . .

2) and a small 0.

3) Attach a
   tear-shaped tail . . .

4) and add a wavy fin.

5) Draw eight lines
   from long to short . . .

6) and three more wavy fins.

7) Make two zigzag lines . . .

8) and a big wavy tail!

Doodle a SAILBOAT with a 4

Catch a quick breeze in a sloop! A sloop is a sailboat with one mast and two sails.

1) Start with a 4 . . .

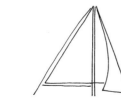

2) add three straight lines . . .

3) and a triangle with one curved side.

4) Draw one straight horizontal line . . .

5) one squiggly horizontal line . . .

6) and attach curved lines at both ends.

7) Set your sails!

5

1) Start with a 5.

2) Add a 3 . . .

3) and attach a long curve.

4) Make a long, curvy 7.

5) Add two curvy paws . . .

6) zig zaggy teeth and stripes.

7) Then finish top to bottom with a nose and tail!

Talk about supersized meals! Tigers can eat as much as 40 pounds of food every day.

Doodle a **TIGER** with a **5**

Doodle a TURKEY with a 6

Hey dude, what's a snood? It's that weird thing on a turkey's beak.

1) Draw a 6 . . .

2) and put a 3 inside.

3) Add five 3's outside and . . .

4) seven more 3's outside that.

5) Draw a small loopy curve on top . . .

6) and a larger curve in front.

7) Shake your tail feathers!

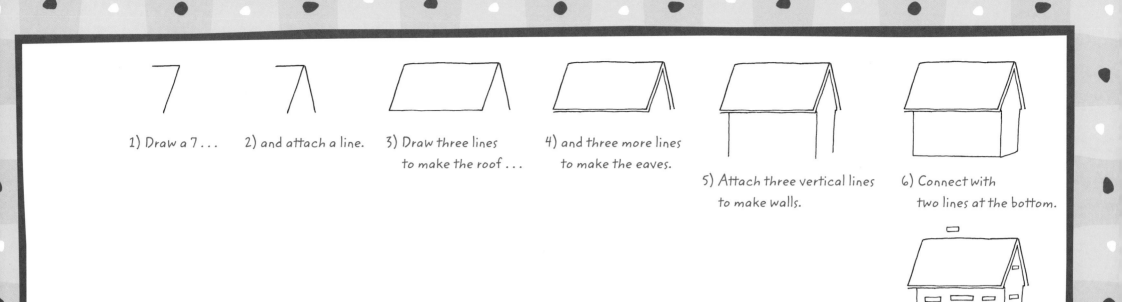

1) Draw a 7...

2) and attach a line.

3) Draw three lines to make the roof...

4) and three more lines to make the eaves.

5) Attach three vertical lines to make walls.

6) Connect with two lines at the bottom.

7) Draw six small boxes...

8) and finish with four windows, a door and chimney.

Doodle a **HOUSE** with a **7**

Usually a house is built from the ground up. But for this house, you'll start from the top and draw your way down.

Doodle a **YELLOW JACKET** with an **8**

These wasps make their nests by chewing wood fibers into paper. Talk about a mouthful!

1) Start with an 8.

2) Put a sideways 8 on top...

3) and two curlicues on top of that.

4) Add a sharp curve on the bottom.

5) Draw two loopy wings...

6) and six double line legs.

7) Add curvy and squiggly stripes.

Doodle a HOT AIR BALLOON

with a 9

To fly a balloon, the pilot lights a burner, heating the air inside the balloon. Because warm air rises, just a little heat gives a big lift!

6) Up, up and away in your beautiful balloon!

5) and connect them.

4) Draw two small boxes . . .

3) and ten lines inside.

2) Add a line on one side . . .

1) Draw a big, fat 9.

Doodle a  LUNCH with a 10

What's for lunch?
Today it's alphabet soup—
or you can draw your
favorite food in the bowl.

1) Draw a 10 with a fat 0.

2) Make the 1 fat, too.

3) Now make the 0 skinny.

4) Draw a bottomless 0.

5) Attach a long loop.

6) Add three curves...

7) and floating letters. Can you find your name?

Doodle and Drawing Fun for Everyone!

Doodles at Dinner $10.99

The original assortment of doodle placemats for dinnertime fun!

Comics to Go $12.95

We start comics, and you finish them! Then you can create your own, from beginning to end.

Doodles to Go
$12.95

Take some doodles on the road: includes a sturdy suface for drawing and a pen. With perforated pages, so you can tear off and display your finished artwork.

blue apple books